from SEA TO SHINING SEA

WASHINGTON

By Dennis Brindell Fradin and Judith Bloom Fradin

CONSULTANTS

John M. Findlay, Ph.D., Associate Professor of History,
University of Washington, Seattle

Robert L. Hillerich, Ph.D., Professor Emeritus, Bowling Green State University;
Consultant, Pinellas County Schools, Florida

CHILDREN'S PRESS
A Division of Grolier Publishing
New York London Hong Kong Sydney
Danbury, Connecticut

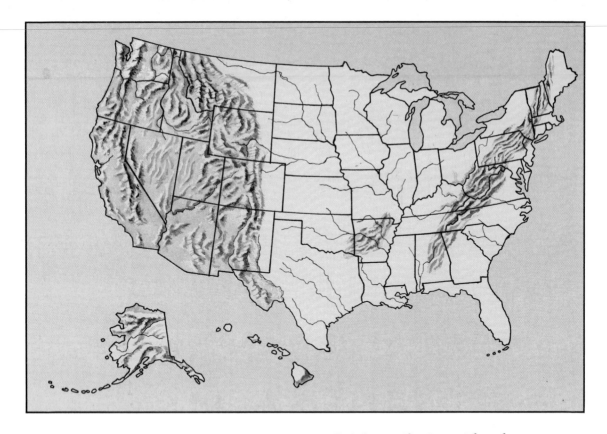

Washington is one of the three states in the region called the Pacific Coast. The other two Pacific Coast states are California and Oregon.

For our cousin Robert Colman, "The Colman Kid"

Front cover picture: The Space Needle and the Seattle skyline at dusk; page 1: San Juan Islands and Orcas Islands; back cover: Coast of Olympic National Park

Project Editor: Joan Downing
Design Director: Karen Kohn
Typesetting: Graphic Connections, Inc.
Engraving: Liberty Photoengraving

Library of Congress Cataloging-in-Publication Data

Fradin, Dennis B.
  Washington / by Dennis Brindell Fradin & Judith Bloom Fradin.
    p.   cm. — (From sea to shining sea)
  Includes index.
  ISBN 0-516-03847-8
  1. Washington (State)—Juvenile literature. I. Fradin, Judith Bloom. II. Title. III. Series: Fradin, Dennis B. From sea to shining sea.
F891.3.F7   1994   94-14549
979.7—dc20   CIP
                                          AC

Table of Contents

A boy and his grandfather at a Wenatchee fruit market

Introducing the Evergreen State

The "Lower 48" means all the states in North America that touch other states. Alaska and Hawaii touch no other states.

Washington is in the northwest corner of the lower forty-eight states (the Lower 48). The state's name honors George Washington. He was the first president of the United States. Washington is called the "Evergreen State." The nickname came from its large forests of beautiful evergreen trees. The green background on the state flag stands for these trees. Washington is also known for its snow-capped mountains.

Rich soil, minerals, and forests attracted early settlers to Washington. Today, large numbers of people continue to move there. The state is a leader in many fields. Washington ranks first in growing apples and sweet cherries. It is a giant producer of lumber and airplanes. Washington is famous for its salmon fishing, too.

The Evergreen State is also well-known for other things. Where is the world's largest building? Where is the country's longest lava tube? Where were Judy Collins and Bill Gates born? The answer to these questions is: Washington!

A picture map
of Washington

*Overleaf: Table
Mountain, in Mount
Baker-Snoqualmie
National Forest*

5

Forests Green, Mountain Peaks, Fields of Wheat

Forests Green, Mountain Peaks, Fields of Wheat

Washington is one of the country's three Pacific Coast states. California and Oregon are the other two. The Pacific Ocean is west of Washington. Oregon lies to the south. Idaho is to the east. To the north is another country, Canada.

Washington covers 68,139 square miles. Its lowest points are along the Pacific Ocean. Other low, level land lies along Puget Sound and the state's rivers. The Columbia Plateau covers most of eastern Washington. Its high, level land is rich for farming. But most of the state is mountainous or hilly. The Olympic, Cascade, and Rocky mountains rise above Washington. The state's highest point is Mount Rainier, at 14,410 feet above sea level.

Washington also has about 600 islands. The largest is 60-mile-long Whidbey Island. There are 172 islands in the San Juan group.

Mount Olympus

Coastal Waters, Lakes, and Rivers

Washington has about 3,000 miles of shoreline. The Strait of Georgia forms part of the state's western

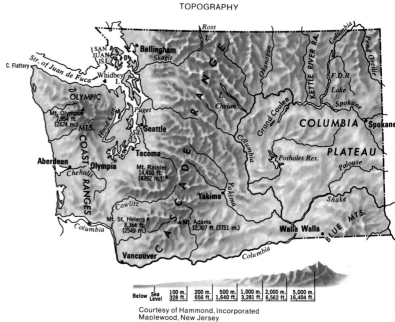

TOPOGRAPHY

Below Sea Level | 100 m. 328 ft. | 200 m. 656 ft. | 500 m. 1,640 ft. | 1,000 m. 3,281 ft. | 2,000 m. 6,562 ft. | 5,000 m. 16,404 ft.

Courtesy of Hammond, Incorporated
Maplewood, New Jersey

border. A big arm of the Pacific Ocean cuts deep into northwest Washington. This is Puget Sound. It is linked to the Pacific by the Strait of Juan de Fuca. Harbors along the sound are important for shipping. Seattle, Tacoma, and Olympia grew around the harbors.

Washington has about 1,000 natural lakes. Snake-shaped Lake Chelan is near the middle of the state. Lake Washington and Lake Sammamish are near Seattle. The damming of rivers created many artificially made lakes in Washington. Franklin D. Roosevelt Lake covers 130 square miles. It is the state's largest lake. The lake was made when Grand Coulee Dam was built on the Columbia River.

Left: Wildflowers in the Cascades, with Mount Adams in the background

9

Left: Woodward
Creek, in the
Columbia River Gorge
Right: A hillside of
phlox in the Columbia
River Gorge

Seastacks on Rialto
Beach, Olympic
National Park

The Columbia River enters northeast Washington from Canada. It winds its way down through the state. Then it flows westward to the Pacific Ocean. Along its course, it forms most of the Washington-Oregon border. The Snake, Yakima, Spokane, and Okanogan are other important rivers.

CLIMATE

The Pacific Ocean warms western Washington in the winter and cools it in the summer. Seattle's temperatures are about 40 degrees Fahrenheit in winter.

About 70 degrees Fahrenheit is common in summer. But the ocean has less effect farther inland. Spokane's temperatures are about 25 degrees Fahrenheit in winter. In summer, they are about 80 degrees Fahrenheit.

Coastal Washington receives rain on more than 182 days of the year. Wet air off the ocean causes this. The wet air falls as rain before crossing the mountains. That is why parts of eastern Washington receive little rain. Those areas are almost like deserts. Winter snowfall is only a few inches near the coast. But it can be 50 to 500 inches in the mountains. Washington also feels the chinook wind. This

Starfish on Second Beach, Olympic National Park

Hoh Rain Forest, Olympic National Park

Oystercatcher

The tallest of these giant hemlocks stands 241 feet tall. The hemlock with the thickest trunk is 28.5 feet around.

Mountain goat

is a winter wind that causes the temperature to rise quickly.

WOODS AND WILDLIFE

Forests cover more than half the state. Some western Washington woodlands receive over 100 inches of rain a year. These areas are called rain forests. The rain helps the trees grow very large. Washington's Olympic National Park has a large rain forest. The country's four largest western hemlocks grow there. The western hemlock is the state tree. The country's two largest noble firs and western red cedars stand in the park. The largest Pacific yew also grows there.

Besides these evergreens, Washington's forests have maples, cottonwoods, aspens, and cherry trees. Ferns and mosses grow in the rain forests. Many pretty wildflowers also grow in Washington. They include dogwood, goldenrod, and brown-eyed Susans. The coast rhododendron is the state flower.

Many kinds of animals live in Washington. Gray whales sometimes approach the Pacific shore. Seals and Dall porpoises often visit Puget Sound. Some of the world's largest octopuses also live in the sound. Washington is famous for many kinds of salmon. The steelhead trout is the state fish. Tuna, flounder,

clams, crabs, oysters, and shrimp also live in Washington waters. Pelicans, blue herons, and puffins fish in the state's waters. Washington's oystercatchers open oysters with their long bills. Peregrine falcons dive at 200 miles per hour from Washington skies. Night herons and northern spotted owls fly about after dark.

Thousands of deer roam Washington. Mountain lions and Canada lynxes prowl about the state. Mountain goats climb through the highlands. Northeast Washington's pine forests are home to the pygmy shrew. It looks like a mouse.

Harbor seals

A hundred pygmy shrews weigh only 1 pound.

13

From Ancient Times Until Today

FROM ANCIENT TIMES UNTIL TODAY

About 50 million years ago, volcanoes erupted along Washington's Cascade Mountains. Lava and ash burst from these cracks in the ground. These materials built up huge mountain peaks. Mount St. Helens, Mount Rainier, and Mount Baker began this way.

Then, about 2 million years ago, the Ice Age began. Glaciers turned northern Washington into a land of ice. During this cold period, mastodons roamed about. So did saber-toothed tigers. The Ice Age ended about 10,000 years ago. Even today, however, glaciers cover some of Washington's mountains.

AMERICAN INDIANS

A few years ago, mastodon remains were found in Washington. A weapon was close by. This meant that people had killed the mastodon. Scientists dated the weapon to about 12,000 years ago. So people have been in Washington at least that long. Those early Washingtonians also left behind tools and cliff paintings.

This glacier is on Mount Olympus

Ice Age glaciers dug holes in Washington. When the ice melted, the holes filled with water and became lakes.

Opposite: Workers loading Washington apples onto a Great Northern train at Wenatchee, about 1915

15

Many of Washington's Indians were known for their beautiful and useful woven baskets and mats.

The chinook wind and chinook salmon were named for the Chinook Indians. Washington is also sometimes called the "Chinook State."

Later, many American Indian tribes lived in Washington. The Cascade Mountains divided them into two groups. The coastal Indians lived west of the Cascades. They built their homes and long canoes with red cedar. Those Indians lived in the same place all year. Salmon was their main food. They also hunted deer and gathered berries. The coastal Indians held potlatches. At these feasts, the hosts gave gifts to their guests. Coastal Indians included the Chinook, Nooksack, Nisqually, and Quinalt.

Other Indians lived east of the Cascades. They included the Spokane, Nez Percé, Colville, Yakima,

16

Okanogan, and Cayuse. Food was less plentiful in the east. So these people moved about to hunt deer and rabbits. They also gathered seeds and roots. They lived in caves that they dug out of hillsides. Later, some of them lived in tents called tepees. Around the 1700s, some of the eastern Indians began to ride horses.

EXPLORERS AND FUR TRADERS

Juan de Fuca claimed to have reached Washington in 1592. He was from Greece but sailed for Spain. The Strait of Juan de Fuca was named for him. In 1775, Spaniards Bruno de Heceta and Juan Francisco de la Bodega y Quadra arrived. Men from their ships were the first Europeans known to have landed in Washington.

Explorer Robert Gray

Captain James Cook was an English explorer. He sailed along the Washington coast in 1778. Another Englishman, George Vancouver, arrived in 1792. His crew explored Puget Sound and the Strait of Georgia. England claimed Washington based on Cook's and Vancouver's visits.

Robert Gray, an American, also explored Washington in 1792. He entered the Columbia River. Based on Gray's work, the United States also

Robert Gray named the Columbia River after his ship, the Columbia. *For many years, all of Washington was known as Columbia.*

Fort Nisqually is a replica of an 1832 fur-trading post. It can be seen in Tacoma's Point Defiance Park.

claimed Washington. In 1803, the United States sent Meriwether Lewis and William Clark to explore the Northwest. They followed the Snake River to the Columbia River. Lewis and Clark then traveled through southern Washington. That November, they reached their goal—the mouth of the Columbia River. Lewis and Clark's trip added to the United States' claim on Washington. At this time, Washington was part of the Oregon Country.

Fur trading had become a big business in North America by the early 1800s. American and English fur traders obtained beaver and other furs from the Indians. The furs were made into clothing. England had fur-trading companies in Canada. One of them was the North West Company. In 1810, this company founded a trading post called Spokane House. Later, the city of Spokane was built nearby. Fur traders from John Jacob Astor's Pacific Fur Company founded Fort Okanogan in 1811. It became the first location in Washington to be occupied by Americans.

In 1818, the United States and England made an agreement. Washington would be open to people from both countries. The Hudson's Bay Company entered Washington in 1821. This English company built Fort Vancouver in Washington in 1825. John

McLoughlin turned this trading post into a town of about 500 people. Later, Fort Vancouver became Vancouver, Washington.

The Indians called John McLoughlin the "White-Headed Eagle." He had a full head of white hair.

THE AMERICAN TAKEOVER

In 1836, Marcus and Narcissa Whitman set up a mission. It was near present-day Walla Walla. They taught Christianity and farming to the Indians. Hundreds of Americans followed the Whitmans to Washington. In 1845, thirty-two Missouri pioneers founded Tumwater. This was Washington's first American town. One of the town's founders was George Bush, a black man. At that time black people were not allowed to own land in Washington. In 1854, a new law was passed. Bush became a landowner. Other Americans settled Olympia in 1846.

In the 1840s, the United States decided to claim part of the Oregon Country for itself. In 1846, England gave up all of its claim to the land south of the 49th parallel.

By this time, some of Washington's Indians feared losing their land to the settlers. The number of Indians had already fallen greatly. Many had died from sicknesses brought by the fur traders and set-

The Whitman Mission National Historic Site

tlers. Some Cayuse Indians blamed the Whitmans for much of this. On November 29, 1847, these Cayuse attacked the Whitmans' mission. The Whitmans and twelve others were killed. Five Cayuse Indians were executed for these crimes.

In 1848, the United States created the Oregon Territory. Washington was part of it. The Washington part alone had 1,200 people by 1850. Seattle was settled in 1851. In 1852, Washington's first newspaper, the *Columbian,* was printed in Olympia. The *Columbian* pushed for Washington to become a separate territory. The United States Congress created the Washington Territory in 1853. Isaac Stevens was appointed governor.

Governor Stevens worked to move the Indians onto reservations. Many coastal Indians signed treaties to give up their land, and so did some eastern tribes. But before reservations were set up, skirmishes broke out between Indians and whites on both sides of the state. The fighting lasted from 1855 to 1858. It was worse east of the Cascades. The Indians had some victories. But the United States Army won in the end. Tribe after tribe was forced onto reservations.

Even more settlers poured in after the Indian wars ended. Some came looking for gold in north-

The settlement of Seattle as it looked in 1860

east Washington. In the 1880s, railroads from the East Coast and Midwest reached Washington. Trains brought still more settlers. By 1889, Washington's population was about 300,000. The United States government made Washington the forty-second state on November 11, 1889.

GROWING LIKE AN EVERGREEN

Before statehood, wheat had been a big crop in eastern Washington. Apples became important there in the 1890s. Other eastern Washingtonians ran cattle and sheep ranches. The fishing industry in Puget Sound grew. Dozens of salmon canneries operated along the Columbia River.

The last rail of the Great Northern Railway was laid in the Cascades on December 10, 1892.

Lumberjacks cutting down a Douglas fir in Washington, 1923

Morning-shift coal miners on their way to the New Castle Slope mines in 1909

The young state's biggest industry was timber, however. Loggers cut down firs and other trees. Lumber from the trees helped build Washington and many other states. By the early 1900s, two-thirds of Washington's workers were in the timber industry.

Washington's early governments helped make life better for Washingtonians. One law set up fair railroad rates for shipping crops. Another law made it safer to work in Washington's coal mines. In 1910, Washington women won the right to vote.

The United States entered World War I (1914-1918) in 1917. In that year, Camp Lewis was begun near Tacoma. Thousands of soldiers received train-

ing there. Altogether, nearly 70,000 Washingtonians served. Many Washington-built ships helped win the war. Washington wheat helped feed many soldiers.

The Great Depression (1929-1939) brought hard times to the country. Many Washington logging camps and factories closed. At one point, one-third of the state's workers were jobless. Poor people in Seattle used crates and boxes to build a town. They called it "Hooverville." Other makeshift towns sprang up around the country. They, too, were called Hoovervilles.

The United States government put many jobless Washingtonians to work. They planted trees and

A Tacoma street scene during the Great Depression

The towns were called "Hoovervilles" because people blamed President Herbert Hoover (1929-1933) for the depression. A Hooverville stood near where Seattle's Kingdome is today.

23

Washington's dams store water that is used to irrigate farmland. Today, most of Washington's electricity comes from power plants at dams.

built roads and dams. Bonneville Dam was completed on the Columbia River in 1938. Grand Coulee Dam was completed on the same river in 1941.

World War II (1939-1945) helped end the Great Depression. On December 7, 1941, Japan bombed America's base at Pearl Harbor, Hawaii. The next day, the United States entered the war. A large number of Japanese and Japanese Americans lived in Washington and in other Pacific states. The United States government thought they might spy for Japan. The government moved more than 100,000 Japanese Americans to special camps. About 13,000 were from Washington. This mistrust

A Japanese American family being evacuated from Bainbridge Island to a camp in California in 1942

was unfounded. When given a chance, Japanese Americans fought bravely for America.

About 250,000 Washington men and women served their country. Hundreds of Washington-built ships helped win the war at sea. The Boeing Company made 13,000 B-17 bombers. The United States government built Washington's Hanford Works in 1943. Workers there made plutonium for two of the first three atomic bombs (A-bombs). In 1945, the United States dropped two A-bombs on Japan. They were dropped from planes made by Boeing. The A-bombs killed about 150,000 people. Yet the bombings helped cause Japan to surrender.

CHALLENGES OF GROWTH

Washington's industries grew after World War II. Aluminum making became a giant business. Boeing began making jet planes. Thousands of new people moved to Washington. Bellevue and other suburbs became big cities in their own right. In the 1970s, electronic companies got started in Washington. So did computer software companies.

Seattle hosted the Century 21 World's Fair in 1962. Nearly 10 million people attended. Seattle's Space Needle became one of the fair's landmarks.

These reporters got a preview of the Hall of Industry at the 1962 Century 21 World's Fair in Seattle.

25

Spokane hosted the Expo '74 World's Fair in 1974. It drew 5.2 million people. Its theme was a clean environment. The Spokane River was cleaned up in time for the fair.

Disaster struck Washington in 1980. On May 18, Mount St. Helens erupted. About sixty people were killed. So were countless deer, elk, birds, and trees. Since then, elk and other animals have re-entered the area. New trees have taken root.

Between 1980 and 1990, Washington's population soared by 735,000. Only seven states gained more people. Most of the growth was around Puget Sound. Rapid growth caused problems. Crime increased. Pollution worsened. By the 1990s, many of Puget Sound's shellfish beds had been damaged.

Shellfish include clams and oysters.

The Hanford Works in southeast Washington had released nuclear waste into the air. By 1990, many people who had grown up in the area were ill. Their cancer rate was unusually high. So was their rate of heart disease. Nuclear materials stored at the site are now being cleaned up. The project will take about thirty years. It will cost more than $50 billion.

Washington's forests have suffered, too. In Colville National Forest, entire hillsides were "clear-cut." This means they were totally stripped of trees. This overcutting of forests hurts animals, too. The

northern spotted owl has lost much nesting area. Only about 3,000 pairs of these birds remain on earth. Logging along the Columbia River has killed some salmon.

The United States government has passed laws to save the trees and wildlife. These laws have helped to cut Washington's logging by two-thirds. Thousands of loggers have lost their jobs. This hurts in a state with a high jobless rate. Even so, many residents agree with these laws. They want the Evergreen State to live up to its nickname.

Clear-cut logging on the Olympic Peninsula

Dams also have hurt the salmon population. They block the fish from swimming upstream to lay their eggs.

Overleaf: A Skagit County organic gardener shows off his carrots.

27

Washingtonians and Their Work

WASHINGTONIANS AND THEIR WORK

There were 4,866,692 Washingtonians in 1990. The state ranked eighteenth in population. But Washington could move up on the list by the year 2000. The state gained about 400,000 people between 1990 and 1994.

Of every 100 Washingtonians, 88 are white. More than one-fourth of them have German ancestors. Many have English, Irish, or Norwegian backgrounds. About 250,000 Washingtonians have Asian or South Pacific backgrounds. Their families came from the Philippines, Japan, China, Korea, Vietnam, Thailand, and Cambodia. Another 250,000 Washingtonians are Hispanic. Most of their families came from Mexico. Washington has almost 150,000 black people. More than 81,000 Washingtonians are American Indians. They live on Washington's twenty-seven reservations and elsewhere throughout the state.

About 250,000 people with Asian backgrounds live in Washington. More than one-fourth of Washingtonians have German ancestors.

HOW THEY EARN A LIVING

Nearly half of Washington's people have jobs. Sales and service work are the leading types of jobs.

A Boeing 757 production line in Renton

About 550,000 Washingtonians sell goods. Nordstrom is a big clothing-store chain. It is based in Seattle. Kirkland is home to Price/Costco. This company runs warehouse clubs. They sell food, clothing, and toys at low prices. Another 550,000 Washingtonians are service workers. They include lawyers and computer servicers. Restaurant, hotel, and hospital employees are service workers, too.

Nearly 350,000 Washingtonians make products. The Boeing Company is based in Seattle. It makes more passenger airplanes than any other United States company. Washington is a shipbuilding leader as well. Only Oregon and California produce more lumber than the Evergreen State. Paper and wood products are other important goods. Washington has long been the country's leading aluminum maker. Milling flour and packaging fish, fruits, and vegetables are other big Washington industries. Microsoft Corporation, based in Redmond, produces computer software.

Aluminum goes into airplanes, soda cans, and aluminum foil.

Nearly 120,000 Washingtonians work in the building trades. Only a handful of states have more builders. About 380,000 Washingtonians are gov-

The lumber industry is important to the state.

ernment workers. Many are teachers. Others work on Washington's military bases. Many people also have jobs in transportation. Airborne Express is a national delivery service. It is based in Seattle.

About 100,000 people work on Washington's 36,000 farms. Washington leads the states at growing apples. About 5 billion pounds of apples are grown there yearly. This comes to about thirty apples for each American. Washington also leads the states at growing sweet cherries, red raspberries, lentils, and hops. Washington ranks second at growing asparagus, potatoes, pears, apricots, and grapes.

Lentils are dried peas and beans used in soups and salads. Hops are used in making beer.

Washington is the country's leading grower of apples.

Halibut being processed at a Bellingham plant

It ranks third at growing green peas and plums. Washington ranks eighth at producing milk. That is its top animal product. Beef cattle, eggs, honey, and broiler chickens are other major farm goods.

Washington is also a leader in the fishing industry. Salmon is one of the state's leading fishing products. Only Alaskans catch more salmon. Crabs, shrimp, oysters, trout, and halibut are also taken from Washington's waters.

More than 3,000 miners work in Washington. They take coal, magnesium, gold, and sand and gravel from the ground.

Overleaf: A Seattle marina

An Evergreen State Tour

An Evergreen State Tour

Washington is a colorful place to visit. It has blue waters, snowy peaks, evergreen forests, and apple orchards. Visitors also enjoy Washington's mountains, historic sites, and pretty towns.

Northern and Western Coastlands

The Peace Arch in Blaine

The Peace Arch is a good place to start a Washington tour. One end of the arch is in Canada. The other end is in Blaine. That is near Washington's northwest corner. The arch honors the friendship between the United States and Canada. Parks are on both sides of the arch. Schoolchildren gave money to build them.

Bellingham is south of Blaine. It is home to the Whatcom Museum of History and Art. Visitors can learn about logging and view Indian baskets there. Bellingham is also known for its scenic views. Mount Baker is to the east. The 172 San Juan Islands are to the west.

Southwest of Bellingham is Anacortes. Ferries head to the San Juan Islands from this town. The

islands are rich in wildlife. Trumpeter swans and eagles can be seen. So can killer whales and Dall porpoises.

On the mainland, south of Anacortes, is La Conner. The Skagit County Museum is in this old fishing town. Children enjoy its lighthouse light and 37-foot Indian canoe. West of La Conner is Whidbey Island. The island has many interesting old towns. Buildings from the 1850s and 1860s still stand in the towns.

West of Whidbey is the Strait of Juan de Fuca. Port Angeles is a vacation town along the strait. It is the entrance to Olympic National Park. The park

This aerial view of Bellingham shows city hall in the foreground and Mount Baker in the background.

covers over 1,400 square miles. Mount Olympus is the park's highest peak. The Blue Glacier can be seen there. Its ice looks clear blue. The park is the rainiest spot in the Lower 48. Its rain forest has the world's greatest variety of giant trees. Marymere Falls is also inside the park. It is a beautiful 90-foot waterfall.

About halfway down Washington's Pacific Coast is Grays Harbor. The harbor was named for its discoverer, Robert Gray. Aberdeen and Hoquiam are twin cities on the harbor's east end. Both are old

Rialto Beach, Olympic National Park

lumber towns. Hoquiam's Castle is a twenty-room mansion in Hoquiam. A rich lumberman built it in 1897. At Aberdeen, visitors can board the *Lady Washington*. It looks like one of Gray's ships.

South of Grays Harbor is Westport. Visitors can charter fishing boats there. The boats also take people offshore to watch for gray whales. Farther south, the coast is dotted with seaside resorts and state parks. Visitors collect shells, dig for clams, and ride horseback across the sand.

Willapa National Wildlife Refuge is near the state's southwest corner. Black brant geese and canvasback ducks can be spotted there. Black-tailed deer, elk, and bears also live there.

CITIES ALONG PUGET SOUND

Everett is near the northern edge of Puget Sound. It is Washington's fifth-biggest city. About 70,000 people live there. Visitors can watch the world's largest passenger planes being put together at the Boeing plant there.

Seattle is south of Everett. Settled in 1851, it was named for Chief Seattle. In 1889, Seattle had a huge fire. When the city was rebuilt, its streets and sidewalks were raised. Parts of some old buildings

The pipe used in Seattle's original water system was made of wood. This section can be seen on the Underground Tour.

The Space Needle

remained beneath the new streets. Today, on the Underground Tour, visitors can see these buildings.

With 516,259 people, Seattle is Washington's largest city. No other Washington city has even half that many people. Trees and other plants make Seattle look very green. That is why it is called the "Emerald City."

Seattle Center is a modern part of the Emerald City. The Century 21 World's Fair was held there. The Center's 607-foot Space Needle looks like a flying saucer on legs. The view is breathtaking from its observation deck. The Pacific Science Center is near the Space Needle. It has displays on water and robots. The monorail carries passengers to and from Seattle Center. It zips along in ninety seconds on a 1.2-mile, single-rail track. The Center's Coliseum is home to the Seattle Supersonics basketball team.

Seattle has something for everyone. Seattle's Aquarium is the only one in the world directly connected to ocean life. Visitors can view life below the surface of Puget Sound. Music lovers enjoy the Seattle Symphony. The Seattle Art Museum has Asian paintings and sculptures. Seattle's International District offers Asian foods and clothing. The Wing Luke Asian Museum has exhibits about Asian folk art. Sports fans watch the Seahawks play football and the Mariners play baseball. Both teams play in the Kingdome.

Tacoma lies on Puget Sound south of Seattle. *Tacoma* was the Indian name for Mount Rainier. It means "big mother to all." Mount Rainier can be seen from Tacoma. With 176,664 people, Tacoma is the state's third-largest city.

Tacoma's Point Defiance Park contains several landmarks. Fort Nisqually is a restored Hudson's Bay Company trading post. Camp Six is an old logging camp. It includes a steam-powered logging railroad and bunkhouses. Children love the park's Never Never Land. Sculptures of storybook characters stand in this woodland setting.

Left: A baseball game at Seattle's Kingdome
Right: A steam-powered engine at Camp Six, in Point Defiance Park

Left: The capitol, Olympia
Right: A meadow in bloom in Mount Rainier National Park

The dome is the same height as the dome of the Capitol in Washington, D.C.

Tacoma is also home to the Washington State Historical Society Museum. Indian and pioneer relics are on view there. Tacoma has one of the world's longest suspension bridges. The 5,450-foot-long Tacoma Narrows Bridge crosses Puget Sound from Tacoma.

Washington's capital is at the sound's south end. Olympia was named for the nearby Olympic Mountains. State lawmakers meet in the Legislative Building. Its dome is 287 feet high. That makes it one of the world's tallest capitol domes. The State Capitol Museum's exhibits tell how Washington became a state.

THE WESTERN INTERIOR

Vancouver is on the Columbia River in Washington's southwest corner. It began as Fort Vancouver in 1825. This makes it Washington's oldest town. Many remains from the fort have been found. They can be seen at the rebuilt fort.

Mount St. Helens is northeast of Vancouver. Visitors can drive around this volcanic mountain. The mountain's Ape Cave attracts many visitors. Lava formed it 1,900 years ago. This 2.5-mile-long tunnel is North America's longest lava tube.

To the northeast is Mount Rainier. Washington's tallest peak is part of Mount Rainier National Park. Mount Rainier's Emmons Glacier is the largest glacier in the Lower 48. The mountain's Paradise Valley is one of the state's many skiing sites.

North Cascades National Park lies in far northern Washington. The park is a wonderland of peaks and mountain lakes. About 320 glaciers are in the park.

THE EASTERN INTERIOR

Yakima, Ellensburg, and Wenatchee are east of the Cascades. Yakima means "big belly." It is in the

Tourists climbing Windy Ridge, on Mount St. Helens

Paradise Valley skiers

heart of apple-growing country. Yakima is home to the Yakima Valley Museum. A pioneer kitchen and blacksmith shop can be seen there. Ellensburg is in cattle-raising country. Each September, the town hosts the Ellensburg Rodeo. Calf roping and Indian dances are part of the fun. Ginkgo Petrified Forest State Park is east of Ellensburg. The park has some of the world's best examples of petrified wood. This

Blossoming pear trees in Peshastin, near Wenatchee

is wood that has turned to stone. Long ago, lava covered the trees and hardened them.

To the north is Wenatchee. It is in another apple-growing area. Each spring, the town hosts the Apple Blossom Festival. Rocky Reach Dam is on the Columbia River near Wenatchee. The dam has an underwater viewing area. From it, visitors can watch salmon heading upstream.

Petrified wood in Ginkgo Petrified Forest State Park

Oroville is an old northeast Washington gold-mining town. When little gold was found, settlers planted apple trees and other crops. To the south was the silver-mining town of Ruby City. When the silver gave out, the people left. Today, a marker shows where Ruby City once stood.

Colville Indian Reservation is east of Ruby City. It occupies much of northeast Washington. The grave of Chief Joseph is on the reservation. This Nez Percé chief tried to lead his people to Canada in 1877. Chief Joseph lived on the reservation from 1885 until his death in 1904. Nearby on the Columbia River is Chief Joseph Dam.

Grand Coulee Dam

Grand Coulee Dam is on the Columbia east of Chief Joseph Dam. This is the world's biggest concrete dam. Grand Coulee Dam is almost 1 mile long. It is the height of a fifty-story building. A glass elevator takes people to the top of the dam.

Franklin D. Roosevelt Lake is behind the dam. Swimmers, boaters, water-skiers, and fishermen enjoy the lake.

Spokane is near the eastern border's midway point. Settlers arrived in 1872. The town they built was named for the Spokane Indians. Spokane now has 177,196 people. It is the state's second-largest city. Spokane is part of the Inland Empire. This includes eastern Washington and parts of Oregon, Idaho, and Montana. Wheat, lumber, and other goods from those states go to Spokane. The city makes foods, wood products, and aluminum.

A waterfall, Spokane Falls, is in downtown Spokane on the Spokane River. The Cheney Cowles Museum highlights the art and history of eastern Washington. It also houses the Northwest's largest collection of Indian relics.

Pullman is north of the state's southeast corner. Washington State University (WSU) is there. Almost 18,000 students go there. It is the second-largest of the state's colleges. Researchers at WSU have developed new kinds of wheat. They have also found ways to recycle wood products.

Walla Walla is west of Pullman. Around it are many streams. *Walla Walla* is an Indian name meaning "place of many waters." Whitman Mission

The University of Washington at Seattle ranks first, with more than 34,000 students.

National Historic Site is near Walla Walla. The Whitmans' mission stood there. Fort Walla Walla Park is also nearby. Fourteen buildings from the fort can be toured.

To the northwest are Pasco, Kennewick, and Richland. Washingtonians call them the "Tri-Cities." McNary Wildlife Refuge is near the Tri-Cities. It is a good place to end a Washington trip. White pelicans, snow geese, and swans are among the birds that can be seen there.

A farm near Pullman

Tri means "three."

A Gallery of Famous
Washingtonians

A Gallery of Famous Washingtonians

Washington has produced many famous people. They include Indian leaders, singers, and sports stars. **Smohalla** (1815?-1907) was born in Washington. He was a Wanapum Indian. Smohalla became a religious leader. He spread the Dreamer religion among the Indians. It urged them to follow the old Indian ways. By doing so, Smohalla believed they could drive the settlers out.

David Sohappy, Sr. (1925-1991) was born near where Bonneville Dam now stands. He was Smohalla's great-grandnephew. Sohappy thought his people should live off the land. American laws restricted this. Sohappy fished out of season. For breaking the law, he was jailed for twenty months. Yet, Sohappy's work improved Indians' fishing rights.

George Washington (1817-1905) was born a slave in Virginia. He grew up in Missouri. In 1852, he came to Washington in a wagon train. He founded Centralia. Today, Centralia has 12,000 people.

Two Seattle natives changed the world of communication. **Chester Carlson** (1906-1968) was a

Opposite: Astronaut Bonnie Dunbar

Dixy Lee Ray

Hank Ketchum with another son, six-year-old Scott

patent lawyer. He spent much time copying drawings of inventions by hand. Carlson felt that there had to be an easier way to do that. In 1938, he invented the photocopy machine. His company became the Xerox Corporation. **Bill Gates** was born in 1955. At the age of nineteen, he was a main founder of Microsoft Corporation. Microsoft became a giant software company. By the age of thirty-seven, Gates was one of America's richest people.

Dixy Lee Ray (1914-1994) was born in Tacoma. Her family owned land on Fox Island in Puget Sound. There, Ray grew to love nature. At the age of twelve, she climbed Mt. Rainier. She was the youngest girl to do that. Later, Ray became a

marine biologist. She taught at the University of Washington (1945-1972). Finally, she served as Washington's first woman governor (1977-1981).

Tom Foley was born in Spokane in 1929. Because he liked politics, his classmates called him "the Senator." In 1964, Washingtonians elected him to the U.S. House of Representatives. He was Speaker of the House from 1989-1994.

Patty Murray was born in Seattle in 1950. She became a secretary and teacher. In 1992, Washingtonians elected her to the U.S. Senate. Murray has worked on issues that concern families. She supports laws for health care, job training, and gun control.

Two famous cartoonists are Washington natives. **Hank Ketcham** was born in Seattle in 1920. Later, he had a son, Dennis, who was always in trouble. "Hank, our Dennis is a menace," said his wife. Ketcham then created the "Dennis the Menace" cartoon strip. As his son grew older, Ketcham gathered ideas from kindergarten classes. **Gary Larson** was born in Tacoma in 1950. As a child, he collected snakes, lizards, and an alligator. He drew pictures of his pets. Animals are among the characters in Larson's "The Far Side." This cartoon appeared in 1,900 newspapers before Larson retired in 1995.

Tom Foley

Dennis the Menace books have sold about 50 million copies. More than 21 million Far Side books have been sold.

Bing Crosby

Judy Collins

Harry Lillis "Bing" Crosby (1903-1977) was born in Tacoma. He grew up in Spokane. He was nicknamed "Bing" because he liked the "Bingville Bugle" comic strip. Crosby became a singer and actor. He won an Academy Award for best actor in *Going My Way* (1944). His recording of "White Christmas" is the biggest-selling record in history.

Musicians **Judy Collins** (born 1939) and **Jimi Hendrix** (1942-1970) were Seattle natives. Collins became a folk singer, activist, and writer. Her hits include "Both Sides Now" and "Send in the Clowns." Hendrix became a rock guitarist. His hits include "Fire" and "Purple Haze." Hendrix died of a drug overdose when he was only twenty-seven.

Ryne Sandberg was born in Spokane in 1959. He was one of the best-fielding second basemen in baseball history. "Ryno" could hit, too. He won the 1990 National League home-run crown. **Earl Averill** (1902-1983) was born in Snohomish. He was an earlier baseball star. Averill smashed a homer the first time at bat in the big-leagues. The "Earl of Snohomish" entered the Baseball Hall of Fame in 1975. **JoAnne Gunderson Carner** was born in Kirkland in 1939. She became a golf champion. Carner won two U.S. Women's Open titles. **John Elway** was born in Port Angeles in 1960. He

became a great quarterback. Elway led the Denver Broncos to three Super Bowls (1987, 1988, and 1990).

Bonnie Dunbar was born in 1949 in Sunnyside. One night when she was in the third grade, Bonnie spotted *Sputnik*. This was a Russian space satellite. Dunbar decided to become an astronaut. In 1985, she was part of a *Challenger* space mission. In 1993, she became the first woman to be honored with the Engineer of the Year award.

Home to Smohalla, Dixy Lee Ray, Bing Crosby, Ryne Sandberg, and Bonnie Dunbar...

The number one grower of apples, sweet cherries, and red raspberries...

Famous also for Mount St. Helens, rain forests, and Grand Coulee Dam...

This is Washington—the Evergreen State!

Chicago Cubs second baseman Ryne Sandberg (left) was born in Spokane. Denver Bronco quarterback John Elway (right) was born in Port Angeles.

Did You Know?

In February 1994, Crystal Mountain set a Washington snowfall record. There, 5.5 feet of snow fell in twenty-four hours. Mount Rainier holds the snowfall record for all of North America. The mountain had 93.5 feet of snow over twelve months in 1971-72.

Walla Walla native Adam West played Batman in the television series of the same name.

Helene Madison of Seattle held every women's swimming record from 100 yards to 1 mile. She also won two gold medals in swimming at the 1932 Olympics.

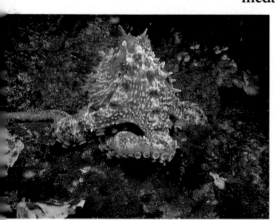

Diver Donald Hagen found a giant octopus in Puget Sound in 1973. The 119-pound octopus measured 23 feet across at the arms.

In the early 1900s, one man claimed the town of Molson. The other citizens moved 1 mile north and started New Molson. The people in New Molson were angry that Old Molson still had the post office. One day when the postmaster was out to lunch, they moved the entire building to New Molson.

The Dungeness crab was named for Dungeness, Washington.

Sonora Louise Smart Dodd arranged for Spokane to hold the first Father's Day on June 19, 1910. She wanted to thank her father for raising a large family alone. Dodd felt that other fathers should be honored, too. The custom spread. Now, each year, the United States and Canada hold Father's Day on the third Sunday of June.

There is a town of George in Washington. The state's other unusually named towns include Humptulips, Concrete, Index, Glacier, Oysterville, Soap Lake, Pe Ell, Tiger, and White Swan.

In 1981, Snohomish County official Tom Murdoch began Adopt-A-Stream. This is a program in which people protect streams from pollution. The Adopt-A-Stream idea has been used as far away as Japan.

The 1980 eruption of Mount St. Helens ripped 1,300 feet off its top. The mountain went from being Washington's fifth-tallest peak to its thirteenth-tallest peak.

Washington is the only one of the fifty states named for a president. The nation's capital, Washington, D.C., also named for George Washington, is a city.

Bertha Landes, elected mayor of Seattle in 1926, was the first woman to be elected mayor of a big U.S. city.

The U.S. Congress officially gave Washington its name in 1853. At the time, however, most people in Washington wanted the territory to be named Columbia.

The team from Kirkland, Washington, won the 1982 Little League World Series by beating Taiwan's team 6-0.

Washington Information

State flag

Rhododendrons

Area: 68,139 square miles (the twentieth-biggest state)

Greatest Distance North to South: 239 miles

Greatest Distance East to West: 370 miles

Borders: The country of Canada to the north; Idaho to the east; Oregon to the south; the Pacific Ocean to the west

Highest Point: Mount Rainier, 14,410 feet above sea level

Lowest Point: Sea level, along the Pacific Ocean

Hottest Recorded Temperature: 118° F. (near Moses Lake, on July 24, 1928; at Ice Harbor Dam near Pasco, on August 5, 1961)

Coldest Recorded Temperature: -48° F. (at Mazama and Winthrop, on December 30, 1968)

Statehood: The forty-second state, on November 11, 1889

Origin of Name: Washington was named for the first president of the United States, George Washington

Capital: Olympia

Counties: 39

United States Representatives: 9 (as of 1992)

State Senators: 49

State Representatives: 98

State Song: "Washington, My Home," by Helen Davis

State Folk Song: "Roll on Columbia, Roll On," by Woody Guthrie

State Motto: *Alki* (a Chinook word, meaning "by and by" or "someday")

Nicknames: "Evergreen State," "Chinook State," "Emerald State"

State Seal and State Flag: Adopted in present form in 1967

State Flower: Coast rhododendron

State Colors: Green and gold

State Bird: Willow goldfinch

State Fish: Steelhead trout

State Tree: Western hemlock

State Gem: Petrified wood

State Dance: Square dance

Some Mountain Systems: Rocky Mountains, Cascade Range, Olympic Mountains, Blue Mountains

Some Rivers: Columbia, Snake, Spokane, Pend Oreille, Wenatchee, Yakima, Okanogan, Skagit, Cowlitz

Some Waterfalls: Marymere, Rainbow, Fairy, Horseshoe

Some Lakes: Franklin D. Roosevelt, Banks, Chelan, Moses, Washington, Sammamish

Wildlife: Whales, sea lions, harbor seals, porpoises, elk, deer, otters, badgers, wolverines, beavers, muskrats, bears, mountain lions, Canada lynxes, mountain goats, wolves, puffins, oystercatchers, peregrine falcons, eagles, owls, herons, ducks, geese, swans, pelicans, many other kinds of birds

Fishing Products: Salmon, halibut, crabs, shrimp, oysters, clams, steelhead trout, cod, flounder, herring, tuna

Farm Products: Apples, sweet cherries, lentils, hops, asparagus, potatoes, pears, apricots, grapes, green peas, plums, wheat, barley, strawberries, peaches, cranberries, onions, dry beans, flower bulbs, milk, beef cattle, eggs, honey, broiler chickens, sheep

Manufactured Products: Airplanes, space-craft equipment, ships, lumber, paper and wooden goods, aluminum, packaged fish and other foods, computers and other machinery, chemicals

Mining Products: Coal, gold, silver, sand and gravel, crushed stone, magnesium, clay, gypsum

Population: 4,866,692, eighteenth among the states (1990 U. S. Census Bureau figures)

Major Cities (1990 Census):

Seattle	516,259	Yakima	54,827
Spokane	177,196	Bellingham	52,179
Tacoma	176,664	Vancouver	46,380
Bellevue	86,874	Kennewick	42,155
Everett	69,961	Renton	41,688

Goldfinch

Western hemlock

Steelhead trout

Washington History

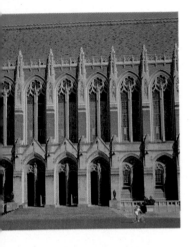

The University of Washington was founded in 1861. This is the university's Suzzano Library.

10,000 B.C.—The first people are known to live in Washington

1775—Members of the exploring expedition of Spaniards Bruno de Heceta and Juan Francisco de la Bodega y Quadra become the first Europeans known to have landed on the Washington coast

1778—James Cook explores Washington's coast for England

1792—American Robert Gray explores and names the Columbia River; Englishman George Vancouver explores the Strait of Georgia and Puget Sound

1805—Meriwether Lewis and William Clark explore Washington for the United States

1811—Fort Okanogan is founded

1818—England and the United States agree that people from both countries can occupy Washington

1825—An English firm, the Hudson's Bay Company, builds Fort Vancouver

1836—Marcus and Narcissa Whitman set up a mission at Waiilatpu near Fort Walla Walla

1846—England gives up its claim to Washington; Olympia is settled

1847—The Whitmans and twelve others are killed by Cayuse Indians

1848—Washington becomes part of Oregon Territory

1851—Seattle is founded

1852—The *Columbian,* Washington's first newspaper, is printed at Olympia

1853—The U.S. Congress creates Washington Territory

1855-58—Washington's Indians fight against whites

1861—The University of Washington is founded

1872—Spokane is settled

1883—The Northern Pacific Railroad links Washington to the eastern United States

1889—On November 11, Washington becomes the forty-second state

1892—Washington State University opens

1899—Mount Rainier National Park is created

1910—Father's Day is begun by Sonora Louise Smart Dodd in Spokane; Washington women win the right to vote

1917-18—Nearly 70,000 Washingtonians serve in World War I

1926—Seattle's Bertha Landes becomes the first woman elected mayor of a big U.S. city

1929-39—During the Great Depression, Washington's logging and manufacturing suffer

1938—Bonneville Dam is completed; Olympic National Park is created

1941—Grand Coulee Dam is completed

1941-45—About 250,000 Washingtonians serve in World War II

1943—The Hanford Works opens to help make the first atomic bombs

1950—The second Tacoma Narrows Bridge is completed

1962—Seattle hosts the Century 21 World's Fair

1974—Spokane hosts the Expo '74 World's Fair

1976—The Kingdome, Seattle's domed stadium is completed

1977—Dixy Lee Ray becomes Washington's first woman governor

1980—Mount St. Helens erupts and kills about sixty people

1989—Happy 100th birthday, Evergreen State; Norman Rice is elected Seattle's first black mayor

1990—Washington's population is 4,866,692

1994—Harold Moss becomes Tacoma's first black mayor; Washington bans smoking in the workplace

The Tacoma Narrows Bridge was completed in 1950

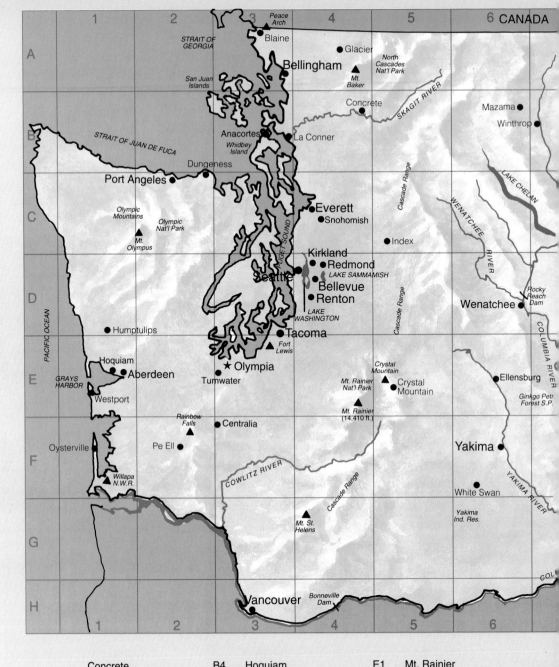

MAP KEY

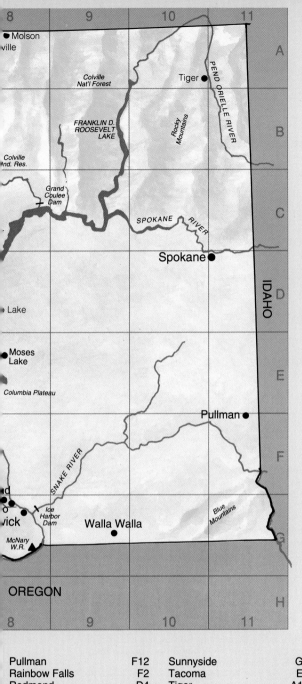

GLOSSARY

astronaut: A person highly trained for spaceflight

billion: A thousand million (1,000,000,000)

capital: The city that is the seat of government

capitol: The building in which the government meets

chinook wind: A winter wind that brings a fast rise in temperature

climate: An area's typical weather

coast: The land along a large body of water

communication: The process of sharing information

depression: A period of hard times with widespread joblessness

evergreen trees: Trees that are always green because they grow new leaves before losing old ones

glacier: A big mass of slowly moving ice

Hispanic: A person of Spanish-speaking heritage

lava: Hot liquid rock from a volcano

61

marine biologist: An expert on the ocean's animals and plants

mastodon: A prehistoric animal related to today's elephants

million: A thousand thousand (1,000,000)

monorail: A train that runs on a single rail

pioneer: A person who is among the first to move into a region

pollution: The harming of natural resources

reservation (Indian): Land in the United States that has been set aside for American Indians

territory: Land owned by a country

transportation: The process of moving things

volcano: A crack through which lava and other materials erupt; a mountain built from eruptions

INDEX

Page numbers in boldface type indicate illustrations.

ABOUT THE AUTHORS

Dennis and Judith Fradin have coauthored several books in the From Sea to Shining Sea series. The Fradins both graduated from Northwestern University in 1967. Dennis has been a professional writer for twenty years, and has published 150 books. His works for Childrens Press include the Young People's Stories of Our States series, the Disaster! series, and the Thirteen Colonies series. Judith earned her M.A. in literature from Northwestern University and taught high-school and college English for many years. The Fradins, who are the parents of Anthony, Diana, and Michael, live in Evanston, Illinois.